CRYPTO-CURRENCIES 101

CRYPTO-CURRENCIES 101

HOW TO MAKE A FORTUNE

FROM DIGITAL CURRENCIES

JAMES ALTUCHER

Published by Laissez Faire Books, 808 St. Paul Street, Baltimore, Maryland
www.lfb.org

Cover and Layout Design: Mena Sugg

CONTENTS

INTRODUCTION:
DON'T BE STUPID

Cryptocurrencies are here to stay. But don't be stupid.

Yes, crypto millionaires and billionaires will certainly be minted in the coming years. There will be plenty of rags-to-crypto-riches stories to go around. And maybe you will be one of them. (If you're reading this, you're an early adopter, so it's possible.) But don't be stupid.

Even the wildest predictions of bitcoin hitting $50,000 by 2020… $100,000 by 2025… or even $1 million by 2034… aren't completely impossible. A few other great cryptocurrencies will rise beyond anyone's imagination, too. But don't be stupid.

I felt compelled to write this book because I'm seeing a lot of smart people suspending their disbelief. I'm seeing a lot of smart people turn stupid.

Cryptocurrencies are great. But I want as many of my readers as possible to avoid the crypto-tulip mania. I want as many people as possible to be less stupid about crypto. Because there's going to be a lot of stupidity in this space — there already is. And I want to live in a less stupid world.

The cold, hard truth, if you can handle it: Up to 99% of the cryptocurrencies that exist today are total SCAMS.

But before you rush off and sell every "sure thing" you've snapped up thus far, read this book. Read it closely.

If you're a regular reader of mine, you might notice some overlap in content in this book from my monthly issues of *The Altucher Report*. That's OK. Cryptocurrencies are complicated. All of it is worth going over at least twice.

It's important to become as familiar as possible with the main points. Especially if you plan to invest in this space. So if I repeat myself, it's for a good reason. Repetition is the mother of mastery.

This book will help you understand this abstract cryptocurrency stuff. It will help you sound more informed at dinner parties. It will help you separate the wheat from the chaff.

Once you realize you can ignore about 98% of what happens in the cryptocurrency space, it becomes far less intimidating.

WHY I WROTE THIS BOOK (EVEN THOUGH I DIDN'T WANT TO)

Obviously, we have lots to cover. Fortunately, I was able to jam a lot — pretty much everything you'll need to know to get started — into this little book.

So let's begin. For starters, here's why I wrote this book:

Every month, many people write me and ask, "What do you think of bitcoin?" Or "What do you think of cryptocurrencies?"

I never wanted to answer.

How come? I believe the first question one should answer is: What did you do for your physical, emotional, creative and spiritual health today?

These are the keys to success. There is nothing else. Wealth is a side effect of applying these ideas every day. So I never wanted to write about something as specific as cryptocurrencies.

Until now. Because I see so many people now talking about cryptocurrencies that are pure scams. I see so many people day-trading these like they are penny stocks.

They are not. And we will get into it in this book. But the rise of cryptocurrencies is part of a 3,000-year-old historical trend in the direction and evolution of money.

It's not a fad. But irrational investors are scooping in and treating it like the latest investing fad. They are going to get burned.

The picture is too familiar. We all saw this in 1997, people flipping penny internet stocks or any company that put the suffix ".com" at the end of their name. It was painful to watch.

Do you know why? Because I also was buying those stocks. I learned my lesson. I started my first internet company in 1995. My job: to actually convince corporations they needed websites and that I should build them.

People didn't realize the internet was not just a fad. Companies like American Express or Time Warner actually had to be convinced to create a website. That this was the future and they needed one.

So there was value in the internet. The internet was here to stay — and it kept growing, into the mobile internet and now the "internet of things." And it's still growing.

But the scams got flushed out. And anyone in them went broke.

The same thing is happening here. The internet was ultimately a multitrillion-dollar opportunity. It's clear now — and you would have been laughed at if you said this then — that many internet companies will be worth well over a trillion dollars.

Apple, Amazon, Facebook, Google, Uber and on and on.

Cryptocurrencies are not just a trillion-dollar opportunity but potentially a hundred-trillion-dollar opportunity or more.

This sounds ridiculous. Again, it sounds laughable.

But there's simple math here. Simply ask: What is the demand for money?

The demand for money is over $150 TRILLION. That's how much money is out there. But currency, as it stands, has many problems. If a currency or idea came along that solved these problems, then the demand for that new idea would be over $150 trillion.

We will describe why and how and what and where: But cryptocurrencies solve the problems created by "regular" currencies. To start: security, privacy, forgery, double-spending, centralized control, risks of inflation and manipulation and on and on.

But let's start with the basics. There's a reason I want to start writing about it. Two reasons, really. But I want to start with the negative first.

98% OF CRYPTOCURRENCIES ARE A SCAM.

Sometimes people ask me, "What do you think of ABC?" where ABC is the latest hot cryptocurrency.

I say, "It's a scam."

They say, "No it isn't."

I say, "Then why did you ask me?"

"Well, why is it a scam?"

And I break open the code and show them where in the code it looks to me like a scam. And I try to explain my philosophy of cryptocurrencies and why if something doesn't fit into that philosophy, I'm willing to bet I can open the code and find out exactly why it's a scam.

My original background is in programming. I wrote my first program in 1982 on an Apple II Plus. I majored in computer science, went to graduate school for it, worked as a programmer for six years and then started software companies for another 12. Even when I traded, it was often based on strategies I tested with software I wrote. And I wrote software to test the strategies.

Do I have experience with cryptocurrencies? I have never written about it before because I never believed it was important to know about how to live a good life.

But again, I see people about to lead a very bad life because of cryptos. And by the way, you can also now live an AMAZING life if you have the right knowledge of cryptocurrencies. Knowledge that I'm going to completely share here in this book as much as I can.

So what is my experience in cryptocurrencies?

In 2013, when bitcoin was a fraction of what it is now, I set up the first online bookstore that ONLY accepted bitcoin. The only book I sold there was my hit best-seller, *Choose Yourself.* This was about a month before I officially released it on Amazon.

CNBC had me on to talk about bitcoin.

My good friend Herb Greenberg, always a skeptic, said, "Did you just do this to get marketing?"

I said, "Where are we?"

"We're on TV. On CNBC."

"I guess it worked."

More recently, several months ago, I was a seed investor in a cryptocurrency I felt was necessary, based on what I felt were the flaws in some of the bigger names.

That cryptocurrency went up 8,000%.

I say all this to establish credentials. We have some time still. Time to figure all this out together and make some money. But I want this section to explain how one should look at the evolution of money and why cryptocurrencies are going to be a part of it.

This will point all of us in the direction of the enormous pockets of opportunity that exist in the cryptocurrency space.

And not just by buying coins.

I want to make this nice and easy for readers. The currencies themselves are very complicated and often difficult to understand. I can explain the philosophy enough here to help people at least avoid the scams.

But I also think people should focus on the public companies — easily traded from a Fidelity account while you sit at your kitchen table — that will benefit the most from this revolution and evolution of money.

Let's begin…

CHAPTER 1:
MONEY IS THE BUBBLE THAT NEVER POPS

I'm going to start at 60,000 feet high.

The good news is this: Cryptocurrencies are super complicated, and most people who talk about them don't understand them at all. And entire books are written about them that are so unreadable and boring it's worthless to buy them and try to understand them.

By the time you finish this book, you will have a great grasp of the way cryptocurrencies work and their potential advantages over traditional currencies.

And very importantly, you'll have an idea of how you can start making money today with this knowledge of cryptocurrencies, even if you don't own any cryptocurrencies and have no plans to.

Cryptocurrencies are true "choose yourself" currencies and fit the trends in every industry I've discussed over the years. There's an evolutionary direction everything's moving in — money is no different. I talk about this evolution in the next chapter.

Theism → Humanism → "Data-ism"

Take any industry: medicine, for example. If you got sick 1,000 years ago (or 5,000 years ago or 20,000 years ago), you'd pray to God (or a god) to save you from this illness inflicted upon you.

Or you'd assume you sinned and were being punished and this was why you were suffering.

That's when medicine depended on theism, a belief that a higher power would solve our problems.

Theism gave way to humanism. We went to human experts instead of shamans or priests. He or she patted our backs until we coughed. Maybe we'd get a little hammer that would hit our knee. And the doctor would say, "Take two aspirin and call me in the morning."

This was fine, but there were so many diseases and illnesses we couldn't solve. And humans are ultimately flawed. George Washington died because doctors thought leeches would suck the illness out of his body. And even now, 250,000 deaths from human malpractice occur each year.

Data solve much of the problem. Instead of the doctor just looking deep into your eyes with a bright light, they now send you over to get an MRI, an EEG or even a genetic test. In the near future, the doctor will feed those data into a database, and the database will then say what likely illnesses you might have, what medicines to take and what surgeries you need, and robots will be part of surgical processes. Average life spans go up every year now.

War, while not an industry, also follows this evolutionary trend.

Three thousand years ago, if two tribes or kingdoms prepared for war, they would pray to their gods. They would have festivals and sacrifices and then go to war. It was assumed that the country with the most powerful gods would win the war.

One of the most sacred texts in Hinduism, for instance, is simply about a war. Who was the winner? The side that had Krishna, the most powerful god.

In every religion, we have seen aspects of this.

Until, again, a few hundred years ago.

Bullets. And people. Humans would decide war. Whoever had more bullets and people on the ground would win the war.

But where is the war now? I will tell you. It's being fought every day all around us. The war is being fought with data.

Every day, some country (guess who) is trying to bring down the electrical grids of Eastern European countries by hacking into their easily hacked older computers.

Again, we saw a whiff of the "data wars," a screenshot but not more, in the U.S. election. Was the election manipulated? Were emails hacked? Of course they were. And that will never stop.

The data wars are in full force. The people reading about them in the newspapers are only reading the rough draft of history. History will eventually be written by the greatest hackers in these wars. The winners.

Money is following this evolutionary path as well. I don't even have to fully describe it.

Take out a one dollar bill.

Look at the back:

"In God We Trust." A leftover remnant of theism. If you can trust God, you can trust this dollar bill.

But even then, trust our Founding Father George Washington and the signature of the secretary of the Treasury. This is a contract! It's not just a piece of paper.

But you have to trust humans to make money in its current form work. And as we will see, humans can make mistakes. And mistakes about money, made by a few humans in charge, can have disastrous consequences that can wipe out entire countries.

Data. "Cryptocurrencies" are the next generation.

Why do I put "cryptocurrencies" in quotes? Because it's a bad word. I don't say that Amazon is a "TCP/IP application." Even though it is.

You don't need to understand the deepest underpinnings of cryptocurrencies to understand why they are important, why the trend is happening and why there is a $150 trillion demand but only $200 billion in supply.

You need to understand what I talk about in this book. This will help you avoid the scams. Get started in the right places. And understand that this trend is only the beginning. No matter how late you think you are in this game, we are still only in the first inning.

But this evolutionary direction is only one aspect.

It doesn't quite answer why cryptocurrencies exist. This boils down to a five-second history of money.

Money has been around, we're learning, for hundreds of thousands of years. But ask 10 people on the street what money is — I guarantee you'll get 10 different answers. (The same can be said about both bitcoin and blockchain, but we'll get there.)

A good answer: Money is the bubble that never pops.

Or Yuval Harari's definition, describing money as a story: "Money, in fact, is the most successful story ever invented and told by humans, because it is the only story everybody believes."

But let's make it easy and bring it down to earth. Why do we have money in the first place?

Two reasons:

A) As a "store of value." You create value in your life. For instance, through savings from the hard work at a job. Or you build a business that has value and you sell it. Or you sell a house.

You created this value and it has to be bottled up somewhere. Like a genie in a bottle. So later you can unleash the value and make all of your dreams come true.

Originally it was resources you simply had on your land. Rice. Wheat. The land itself.

Later it was metals. Gold is often talked about as a "store of value." But it's not. It's a rock.

Gold has some intrinsic value. It can be used as an electric conductor, for instance. It has antibiotic properties. It probably has about $60 in intrinsic value. The rest of the value is that for millennia, people have relied on it as a store of value.

People buy necklaces or rings or other jewelry not only as ornaments but as convenient ways to travel with this store of value.

And for a long time, gold was used to back paper currency. Until everyone decided that "In God We Trust" seemed to have even more extrinsic value than the metal itself.

And bitcoin is a store of value. A great example is to see the correlation in the price of bitcoin with any government change in Argentina. Argentina is known for being a horrible country as far as how they treat their currency. They have had hyperinflation, the government has seized money directly out of bank accounts, there is a black market, there is even something called a "blue market."

The currency is a mess. And whenever it looks uglier than usual, bitcoin spikes.

How come? Because the wealthy have gotten smarter. They know they can't rely on their currency, or even gold, to get their wealth out of the country in an emergency. So they use bitcoin.

This is the canary in the coal mine. A clue as to what will come. Argentina, in its wretchedness, has pointed toward the future.

As our faith in humans disappears, our reliance on stable and trustworthy data will rise.

B) To pay for things. And to sell things. First there was barter. But think about the problems of this. For every two items, people had to figure out what the items were worth relative to each other.

If I had a pair of shoes and wanted an apple, how many apples would I get for a pair of shoes? But what if I had only one pair of shoes (I'm a cobbler), and I want an apple and some milk. Do I need to cut my shoes in half?

And with hundreds of possible items to barter, that's tens of thousands of exchange rates. It's too complicated.

Money made out of hard-to-get metal became a common store of value that can be easily traded because one side of the transaction always has the same value. So negotiation became much easier.

Again, I said, "One side of the transaction always has the same value." But that all depends. What if supply went up and nobody told us?

Well, that's a BIG problem cryptocurrencies solve. And we'll get into all of the pros (and cons) of crypto in a moment.

First, here's the evolutionary direction that everything in the world is moving in. It answers why the rise of cryptocurrencies is just an inevitable and natural evolution of money.

CHAPTER 2:
WHY THE RISE OF CRYPTO IS INEVITABLE

"Bitcoin is almost to computers what quantum mechanics is to physics."
— Naval Ravikant

I spoke about the evolutionary trend in every industry: theism (a belief that a higher power will solve our problems) to humanism (a belief that humans will solve our problems) to data-ism (a belief that data will solve our problems).

But now let's look at the trends and problems in money. From barter to precious metals to government-controlled currencies to where we are now.

We will see that even in the history of money, and not just the evolution of every industry, the demand for a data-based currency solves critical problems that must be addressed in the decades and generations ahead.

CRYPTO IS A NATURAL EVOLUTION OF MONEY

Human error, frailty and weakness will be the downfall of traditional currency, and it has already begun.

Think about it this way:

James wants to send money to Joe.

Many things have to now happen.

James tells his local bank. They tell the local reserve bank. They tell the Federal Reserve (who quietly tells the IRS). The Federal Reserve tells the central bank of Joe's country, who then tells Joe's local bank. And finally Joe goes to his ATM and takes out the money.

Well, let's break down what just happened:

A) Six discrete steps occurred. There was the possibility of human error at every step. There were also transaction costs at every step. These transaction costs are the built-in inflation of a centralized banking system.

B) James and Joe lost all rights to the privacy of the value they have spent their lives creating (note: IRS or NSA or FBI or CIA or DEA or DIA). Maybe it doesn't matter to them. But sometimes it does.

C) Not only is human error a risk, but humans controlled the value they sent. Hidden transaction costs are baked into every step of the system. And there's also the various "black boxes" inherent in centralized banking systems: For instance, how much new money is the Federal Reserve printing today?

We simply don't know. They don't tell us every way in which they create new money without permission.

Value is determined by supply and demand. What happens to the value of your hard-earned money if people you don't know and have no faith in are completely deciding supply (and then value) without your knowledge or permission?

THE PHILOSOPHY OF CRYPTOCURRENCY

I'm not a money conspiracy theorist. These issues have always existed and they have toppled empires, but so far the United States has proven superior to the fallen and forgotten. Hopefully that will always be true.

But history says it won't always be true. When and where and why and how is not known.

All we know is direction.

Direction is the philosophy of cryptocurrencies.

FIVE MAIN PHILOSOPHIES OF CRYPTO

With bitcoin, there are thousands of copies of the blockchain running all around the world. Anyone who has a copy of it can do a full validation of the transactions in the full chain.

Historically, it was the central bank that validated the transactions. Now, blockchain allows everyone on the network to have a copy — and autonomously validates all of the transactions together.

You can see how this eliminates not only the need for a central bank — but also the need for human intermediaries at all.

Let's look at the five main philosophies of a cryptocurrency:

1. Security: If James sends money to Joe, Joe gets it.

2. Decentralized: There are no geographic borders to the currency.

3. Anonymity: Nobody needs to know about my transaction.

4. Forgery: This is really the same as "A" but in some situations is slightly different: If James sends money to Joe and Joe sends money to Bob, Bob can trust that the money is not forged by someone along the way. There is no "duplicate money."

5. Controlled supply: It should always be known by every party how much supply exists and under what conditions supply would stop and, in probably every case, whether supply has a maximum. For instance, the maximum number of bitcoins that will ever be mined is 21 million bitcoins.

DATA-ISM AND MONEY 2.0

There is another aspect of cryptocurrency that has never before been seen in civilization. This aspect exists only because of the rise of data.

You can make a currency that also has a function (much like an app on a phone).

I'm not going to get into the details of that right here because I want to stick to the basics. But I will talk about it in *Crypto Corner*.

I will say this...

Possible applications in the cryptocurrency space (meaning the functionality is built into the data itself) include data storage, the internet of things (IoT), digital health care, escrows and wills and on and on.

CHAPTER 3:
THE GOOD, THE BAD, THE UGLY

OK. Now that you've seen the big picture, let's drill down.

As I said in the last chapter, cryptocurrencies are just the natural evolution in money. And there are plenty of reasons to look forward to their rise.

Great as they are, they won't solve all of our problems. They'll just create new problems for us. And we'll get smarter as a result.

In this chapter, we'll look at the anatomy of cryptocurrencies. We'll begin with a transaction, then look at the good, the bad and the ugly sides of cryptocurrencies. And why there's a solution for every "bad."

First, let's take a look at what happens in a crypto transaction.

ANATOMY OF A CRYPTO TRANSACTION

Cryptocurrencies, as the name suggests, are protected by cryptography. Historically, cryptography was the art of keeping secrets from your enemies using mathematics — or at least attempting to. Like the Enigma Machine. Except the Nazi's cryptography was nothing like what we have today. It was weak.

Today, for the most part, the methods Alan Turing used to crack the

Enigma are worthless. Our cryptography today is very strong.

The type of cryptography bitcoin uses (called "one-way hash func-tion") is like a one-way digital portal — or a digital trapdoor. You can put data through it and the cryptographic function (complex math formula) transforms it into something incredibly unfamiliar from its original state. So unfamiliar that it's impossible to undo by working backwards.

It's easy to get from A to B. But without the "key" to unlock the data (and solve the math problem), it's very, very difficult to get from B to A. That's what keeps your data safe.

WHAT A CRYPTOCURRENCY TRANSACTION LOOKS LIKE

What does a cryptocurrency transaction look like?

- James wants to send money to Joe
- He puts together a "transaction" on his computer that describes how much he wants to send.
- The transaction is added to a "block"
- The "block" is sent all over the network and the network "validates" the transaction by looking at all the prior transactions that led to James having enough validated currency.
- The currency is sent to Joe.

The transaction is now there in the block. And Joe is now in control of his own "private key" that controls the funds.

Cryptography protects Joe's funds from **A)** being duplicated and **B)** being stolen from him. As long as Joe takes reasonable security measures (I'll show you how in **Chapter 5**), his crypto will be safe.

Each new block created on this chain of blocks (hence, "blockchain") adds yet another layer of difficulty, making it harder and harder to reverse each "one-way" cryptographic problem. Thus it becomes exponentially more difficult to change the validation of James' transaction, the more blocks are added.

Famed cryptographer Nick Szabo likened this process to a fly getting trapped in amber. The more time passes by, the more the amber accumulates and the harder and harder it gets to remove the fly from the amber. So a block can be likened to another thin layer of digital amber and the blockchain is the collective depth of the digital amber. Something like that.

WHAT IS A BLOCKCHAIN?

A blockchain

A) guarantees the correctness of its past and present data

and

B) guarantees the correctness of its future state and data

Blockchains replace intermediaries with mathematics. Before blockchains, digital currencies had to run through central servers and be logged by central bookkeepers. Your money had to rely on several single points of failure before it would reach your intended destination.

Blockchain solved that problem.

This is all greatly oversimplifying. But it's useful. And it's a good starting point for understanding crypto.

So zooming out, here's what all of this really means in a nutshell:

- **No geographic borders**

- **No banks**

- **Anonymity** (in bitcoin, the size of the transaction can be seen, but James' and Joe's names can't be seen. In other cryptocurrencies, there might be much greater anonymity)

- **The validation (much like a deli clerk checking to see if a $100 bill is forged) is done by computers** that raise their hands and say, "We are miners and will do it for free." The miners don't charge transaction costs, but depending on how the currency is designed, they might get more coins depending on how much "work" they do to validate transactions

- **Decentralized.** Which is part of the privacy of the transaction and also ensures that no one source is controlling the validation (and then possibly faking transactions or minting more money).

Now there are several obvious pros here that I've already alluded to in **Chapter 2**. But there are also downsides to these points. So let's talk about those.

THE MANY PROS AND CONS OF CRYPTO

We'll start with the good this time.

The good:

A) A standardized and neutral confirmation policy backed by software that has no human agendas.

What does this mean?

Imagine I want to send Joe dollars to buy his house. I need to trust all of the middlemen between Joe and me: local bank, central bank, lawyers, governments, Joe's bank, etc., to approve of this transaction if I do it in dollars.

This is OK, but at each step, someone could be untrustworthy. They are all humans, even the government (humans subtly influence the price of the dollar and also share details of the transaction with unfriendly parties (the IRS)).

Also, each step in the above has a transaction cost. So inflation is built into the system.

If this were a bitcoin transaction, enough miners need to approve that this transaction is valid. So even if a few miners are not trustworthy, the bulk of them will be, and we can trust that the transaction between Joe and me is legit.

This is the ENTIRE reason for cryptocurrency: to avoid governments, borders, middlemen and extra transaction costs. As well as have high security and avoid forgery.

(There is another reason for cryptocurrency, which is to do more complicated transactions that we can call "contracts" (also known as "smart contracts" without lawyers, etc.) This reason is sometimes the basis for legit ICOs. We'll get into that later.)

This was also originally the entire reason for the origin of money as opposed to a barter system (which requires an exponential number of negotiations to determine the correct exchange rates between each object).

Crypto is just the next step after that.

For bitcoin, the cost might be zero (depending on your exchange), and miners get paid by getting more bitcoin depending on the computation power used to verify these transactions.

One more good: Blockchains are incredibly resilient. A blockchain can survive unaffected as long as just one stays alive. So if there's a catastrophic failure throughout the nodes, it takes just one lone survivor to keep the network running without any loss of data.

With bitcoin, nodes are running all over the world. The power is distributed. There's no single vector of attack. To kill it, you have to eradicate it completely, globally, totally, without fail, all at once.

This is very hard to do. It's why bitcoin is incredibly strong — the most secure network on Earth.

The bad:

Miners approve transactions one block at a time. A block is a set of transactions. A "blockchain" is a chain of these timestamped blocks. If a transaction doesn't make it into one block, it waits a certain period of time to get into the next block. So there's lag.

Blockchains are slow.

Blockchains are slow because blockchains are extremely inefficient — especially compared to Visa, MasterCard or PayPal. There's a reason. Decentralization and censorship-resistance. That's what sets Bitcoin apart from traditional payment systems and inefficiency is the trade-off.

Blockchains are inefficient.

Another "bad" is that everyone can see the transaction (on bitcoin) although nobody knows it was Joe and me involved in the transaction.

Blockchains aren't inherently anonymous.

Another "bad" is that for certain types of transactions (buying a cup of coffee), the blockchain allows for a layer of software above it to quickly verify before the blockchain protocol validates the transaction... or software to provide other services on the blockchain (e.g. a bitcoin exchange that stores wallets for people).

That software layer involves humans (humans are bad), which invites good players and bad players to be involved (hence, the Mt. Gox $400 million theft).

Blockchains are very hard to scale.

In exchange for security, trust, fewer middlemen and avoidance of governments and boundaries, society pays in computational costs, storage (the same blockchain stored on millions of computers is a waste) and slower transaction speeds. And the software layer above the blockchain needs to evolve, which it is (the same way internet software evolved post 1991).

FOR EVERYTHING BAD, THERE ARE SOLUTIONS

For all of these problems ("the bad" described above) there are solutions.

This is the ENTIRE reason multiple currencies exist and why there is a huge need to keep things simple and not get caught up in the hype.

Coins can be divided into two types:

A) They keep the same rough philosophy of bitcoin (security, limit on minting of new coins, elimination of middlemen and boundaries, validations of trades, impossible to forge).

and

B) NOT the above (scams that pretend to be "A," but there are backdoors available to bad players).

As you'll see in the next chapter, most cryptocurrencies on the market are B) — they are scams. But that doesn't mean you shouldn't pay attention to the "altcoins." The cryptocurrency space needs more than just bitcoin.

I'll tell you why.

CHAPTER 4:
ONE COIN TO RULE THEM ALL? NO. ("ALTCOINS" EXPLAINED)

There's bitcoin, ether, ripple, dash, blah, blah, blah. Anything that's not bitcoin is often referred to as an "altcoin." People who love bitcoin and hate altcoins sometimes call themselves "bitcoin maximalists." They believe bitcoin is the only true cryptocurrency — and everything else is a scam.

To their credit, they're not completely wrong.

Of the close to 1,000 cryptocurrencies out there, about 90–95% are complete Ponzi schemes and will eventually go to zero. That's just the truth.

Unfortunately, the only way to know this is to read the code, and there are hundreds of thousands of people using these currencies right now, unaware of the trap they are in.

But that doesn't mean the bitcoin maximalists are completely right, either.

So… why more than one? Why didn't they stop at bitcoin?

Well, for one, it's extremely easy to create a new currency. You don't even need to know how to code. You can be a teenage "script kiddy" and just copy and paste the bitcoin code, slap a new logo on a Wordpress page and *voila*.

For example, here's all you need to create a new token on the ethere-um platform:

You could just copy and paste this into a new contract in the ethereum wallet and create your token in minutes. (If you don't know what any of this means, don't worry. We'll get to how ethereum works in **Chapter 5**.)

```
contract MyToken {
        /* This creates an array with all balances */
        mapping (address => uint256) public balanceOf;
        /* This initializes contract with initial supply tokens to the creator
of the contract */

function MyToken(
        uint256 initialSupply
        ) {
        balanceOf[msg.sender] = initialSupply;
// This gives the creator all initial tokens
 }
 /* Send coins */
 function transfer(address _to, uint256 _value) {
        if (balanceOf[msg.sender] < _value) throw; // This checks to
see if the sender has enough
        if (balanceOf[_to] + _value < balanceOf[_to]) throw; // Check
for overflows
        balanceOf[msg.sender] -= _value; // Subtract from the sender
        balanceOf[_to] += _value; // Add the same to the recipient
}
```

If you know how to code, you can customize it to your specifications. Or you can just copy and paste from other currencies and add features you like. It doesn't really take much more than that.

And the thing is…

As time goes on, it'll only get easier to make and customize, your own cryptocurrency. Sure, most of them will be useless.

But there's a good reason to have them around. I don't think there will be "One Coin to Rule Them All." And I don't think that's a practical idea. I think there will be many winners.

Data-based currency is an important evolution. And the children inherit traits from the parents.

Let's look at today's paper currencies. There are many valid currencies. For instance, there are "dollars" and "euros."

Why are there two?

Because dollars are in America and euros work in Europe. This is based on the arbitrary and fictional geographic borders that were set up through human-led trade agreements, wars, etc.

With cryptocurrencies, there are no geographic borders. Bitcoin and ether, for instance, work just as well in every single part of the world.

New cryptocurrencies develop for two AND ONLY TWO valid reasons (in my opinion based on years of studying this).

TWO REASONS CRYPTO EXISTS

A) To solve a problem in the currency. For instance, upon writing this book, bitcoin is very slow to validate a transaction. So it's hard to buy a cup of coffee with it (there are a lot of technical details on this, but it is a legitimate problem of bitcoin).

Someone can work on the software and say, "Ahh! I found a possible solution." They can then implement the currency and if the solution works, their currency might get more popular and get used for those types of transactions that require speed.

Another problem: privacy. Bitcoin transactions have privacy. But not total anonymity since every transaction is stored (without names) on what is called "the blockchain."

Many currencies have developed to help solve this problem.

Legitimate problems in certain cases and a lack of geographic borders are what create new cryptocurrencies.

B) A data-based currency can have some functionality. It's like traditional currency mixed with apps.

For instance, there is a coin (full disclosure: I own some) called file-coin that creates peer-to-peer storage. What does this mean? Let's say you store data on Dropbox or Google Drive.

That's not Peer to Peer. Your data sits on servers owned by Google or Dropbox. There is a potential for human error and privacy loss. A crypto-currency in which transactions include the ability to allow people to store data with your currency (and allowing you to get more currency if you let your "digital wallet" be used in this way) solves a problem.

Again, problems in specific use cases are the "data boundaries" that have replaced geographic boundaries.

This is a lot for this introduction.

But it gets to the heart of the matter and I can sum it up:

- Cryptocurrencies (or, I almost prefer, data-driven currencies) are here to stay and only going to get bigger.

I will describe the size of the opportunity in a future issue.

- 95% of currencies are scams. How come? Because in any eupho-ria, criminals are created. We saw it with internet stocks in 1999; we saw it with hedge funds in the 2000s; we saw it with mort-gage-backed securities in 2008 and now we are going to see it in cryptocurrencies within the next year or so.

But the industry itself will boom.

This was a lot for one issue. And cryptocurrencies are a very compli-cated subject. Like I said, to actually know for sure if a cryptocurrency is legitimate or not, the only way is to read the actual software that created it.

The good news is that, unlike the dollar, the software is available. And I've read it.

WE NEED NEW CRYPTOCURRENCIES

Unless they're blatant scams, new coins and/or a fork in bitcoin are at-tempts to solve the above problems. There is NO SINGLE solution. Many solutions may exist, hence the reason why there may be more than one winner as cryptocurrency evolves.

Analogy: America has "dollars." Mexico has "pesos." In human currencies, both currencies have "won."

The "problem" solved above is that Americans might trust the U.S. government and Mexicans trust the Mexican government. Geographic boundaries create new currencies. But geographic boundaries are man-made and artificial, and many possible untrustworthy middlemen are required.

In crypto terms, "zcash" might be used for transactions requiring high anonymity. "Filecoin" might be used for transactions that have a specific storage application.

In other words, "crypto boundaries" are determined by real problems being solved rather than artificial geographic boundaries.

CHAPTER 5:
BUYING, SELLING & SECURING YOUR COINS

You can buy cryptocurrencies from a number of exchanges. The ones I recommend you take a look at are:

A. **Coinbase** — the most mainstream option. Certainly the most established. Buying and selling is easy and your bitcoins are insured. (Learn more about Coinbase on their Support page: **https://support.coinbase.com/**) **With Coinbase, you can purchase bitcoin, litecoin and ethereum.**

https://www.coinbase.com/

B. **Kraken** — Another great choice. Kraken is known for its security, support and low fees. Signing up and getting started is simple. **Plus, it provides a few more options to choose from: ethereum (ETH), monero (XMR), dash (DASH), litecoin (LTC), ripple (XRP), stellar/lumens (XLM), ethereum classic (ETC), augur rep tokens (REP), Iconomi (ICN), melon (MLN), zcash (ZEC), dogecoin (XDG), tether (USDT), gnosis (GNO) and Eos (EOS).**

https://www.kraken.com/

These exchanges are very easy to use. If you can use PayPal or online banking, you can figure these out fairly quickly.

STORING YOUR COINS

Another question I get a lot is how to secure your cryptocurrencies. First things first, don't keep your coins on the exchanges — which are basically just centralized, unregulated online banks.

Cryptocurrencies are the first form of money you can store in your brain. That's a revolutionary idea. But right now, it's also pretty involved. It's a long process. It'll get easier. But now, it's not.

But even if you don't want to store your bitcoin in your brain, it's best practice to always have control of your private keys.

Let me unpack what I mean by that.

PUBLIC VS. PRIVATE KEYS

Your cryptocurrencies come with both a "public key" and a "private key."

Your public key is your address. It's what you give to people who want to send you money.

Your private key is, put simply, your account "password." When a transaction is executed, you "sign" the transaction with your private key. Your private key unlocks your funds.

When you hold your cryptocurrencies in exchanges, you don't own the private key. The exchange does.

One great thing about cryptocurrencies is you can become your own banker — so keeping your crypto on an exchange defeats this purpose. It also goes against the idea of decentralization — centralized exchanges can't be trusted. They have one vector of attack and, if hit hard enough, they come crashing down.

So how do you secure your coins (private keys)?

I'll talk about three ways in this chapter.

A. Store them in a downloadable "hot" wallet specific to your coin [easy, less secure]

B. Store them in your brain [very difficult, very secure]

C. Store them in your safe, hidden compartment or in a fake can of hairspray buried in your backyard [somewhat difficult, highly secure]

D. Store them in a cold wallet device [moderately easy, very secure]

THE DOWNLOADABLE "HOT" WALLET

Most currencies have their own "wallets" you can download and hold your coins on your computer or smartphone.

If you want a bitcoin wallet, for example, you can download it here: **https://bitcoin.org/en/download**

But what if you want a wallet for a different cryptocurrency? Well, sorry to send you off, but the easiest method, as usual, is to Google it. **(Google: "download [cryptocurrency name] wallet")**

But wallets aren't without risks. The security of your coins is as strong as the security of your device.

So if you're going to go with this method, I suggest using a VERY strong password and having several backups. (encrypted USB sticks and external hard drives.)

If you want maximum security, I suggest you either:

A. Secure your money in your brain

B. Secure your money in your safe

C. **(Most recommended)** Secure it in a cold-storage wallet device (although this choice is limited to a few coins).

I'll go through all of these one by one.

But before I do, if you're an ABSOLUTE beginner, I'd suggest you just skip to C and get a cold-storage wallet device. They are pretty plug-and-play and they're easily the safest way to store your coins.

Remember: The reason crypto exists is so you can better control your own money. If you don't hold it, you don't own it.

The best way to secure your bitcoins for mid- to long-term storage is to put them in "cold" storage.

Meaning, get them off of online exchanges and into an account where the private key has never been exposed to the Internet. ("Hot" wallets are those connected to the Internet and vulnerable to attacks.)

Thus, it's virtually impossible to fall into the wrong hands online. (And as long as you secure it properly, it'll be safe in the physical world, too.)

1. How to create a brain or paper wallet

Cryptocurrencies are the first form of money you can store in your brain.

There are many ways to do this. But I'm going to show you a secure way that won't be too confusing. This process can get extremely complicated. Here's a very simple way to do it.

First step: **Go to WarpWallet.** (Link: **https://keybase.io/warp**)

2) Right-click anywhere on the web page and click "Save as"

3) Turn off your Wi-Fi, find the file you just downloaded and open it. (You don't want to be connected to the Internet when you create your private key.) If you want to be SUPER SECURE (recommended), put the file on a clean thumb drive, move it to a computer that's never been connected to the Internet, open it up, then follow the instructions below.

You should be shown the same page.

4) Put in a REALLY, REALLY strong password in the "passphrase" field. And put an email in the email box. (You can put in your regular email, but I recommend creating an email JUST for this purpose with 2FA enabled.)

I want to reiterate the importance of a strong passphrase. Anything below 14 characters and with familiar phrases is susceptible to a "brute force" attack. Meaning, given enough time, hackers could figure it out by testing out every possible combination of characters. Strong passwords are meant to make this process as cost-prohibitive and time-intensive as possible.

The problem people will run into with bitcoin is because they'll be expected to manage their own security, they'll goof it up. They won't put enough effort or thought into the small portion of security left up to them — securing their private keys effectively.

5) Click "Generate" and watch it work its magic.

Once generated, you'll be presented with these:

From here, you have a choice.

6.) Write down or print your private key — or don't.

This is where you have to decide whether you're going to create a brain wallet or a paper wallet.

The purpose of a brain wallet is not having a paper trail. If you are 100% confident in your ability to remember your passphrase, don't write it down.

If you're only 99.9999% confident in your ability to remember it, write it in coded form. Write it in your journal, coded within every seventh word. Write it in a book by circling the letters on every third page. Get creative.

Or just write it down and keep it in a VERY safe place.

If you do this, you've moved from a brain wallet to a paper wallet.

If you go the paper wallet route, you have two choices:

1. You could write down/print your passphrase and email.

2. You could cut to the chase and write down/print your private key and/or copy your QR code. (Your QR code will make it easier to spend your funds in the future.)

In the end, your private key is what you're after. Your private key/QR code is what you'll use to access your funds in the future. (More on that in a moment.)

Whatever you do, I suggest writing or printing out your passphrase/ private key down in three separate places and putting those pieces of paper in safe places. One inside your home. One outside your home. And another elsewhere.

You decide. You know best.

YOUR PUBLIC KEY

Copy your "public key" and paste it somewhere safe on your computer for easy access. This is where you'll send your bitcoins.

You'll want to keep this relatively safe.

Important: The privacy risk in other people knowing your public key is they can look up how much money you have on that particular address. Something to keep in mind.

7.) Destroy all evidence before you log back in.

Once you're ABSOLUTELY SURE you've got the right private key, hit "Clear and reset." Poof. It's gone.

8.) Send your bitcoins to your "public bitcoin address."

I suggest sending only a little bit first, to prove it works.

Copy your public bitcoin address and go to your chosen exchange (Coinbase, Kraken or whatever you choose). Under the "send" function, this is where you'll send the bitcoin. (**Pro-tip:** Always send a tiny bit on your first go to ANY address to test it out. AND always check then double-check to make sure the public key is YOUR public key. If your computer is compromised, hackers can replace your address with theirs in your clipboard.)

9.) Access and spend your bitcoins

If you chose the brainwallet option, simply open up your Warp Wallet again (preferably offline) and enter your passphrase and email. Grab your private key. (I'll tell you what to do with it in a moment.)

If you chose your paper wallet, you already have your private key. Get it.

Claiming the funds requires specific software. This software is a type of "hot" wallet. "Cold" wallets, like your brain or paper wallets, are wallets stored offline. "Hot" wallets are the opposite — stored online.

To spend your coins, you'll have to move your coins to a "hot" wallet. There are varying degrees of safety when doing this. Again, I'll show you two simple and secure ways.

1. The first is a way to put ALL of your funds on a web wallet.

2. The second is a way to do a partial spend in which the wallet destroys your private key when the transaction is over, keeping the remaining funds secure.

HOW TO CREATE A WEB WALLET

Visit **blockchain.info** (**https://blockchain.info/wallet/#/signup**) to start a new Web wallet. An email address is optional but helpful for recovering your account should the need arise.

Create a password. (Pro tip: Use a password manager like LastPass to create a 100-character password with uppercase and lowercase letters, numbers and special characters.)

You'll be directed to this page. Let's get your security measures out of the way first. For added security, go to "Settings" on the sidebar. Click it.

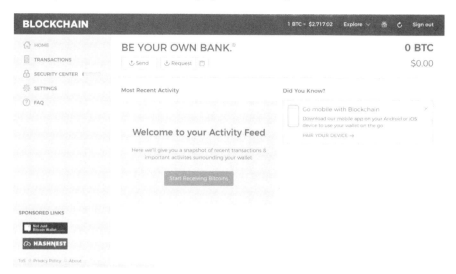

A page with your "Wallet information" will open up. Save your Wallet ID in a safe place. It is your "username" to log in to your wallet. (You can save it into your password manager as "username.")

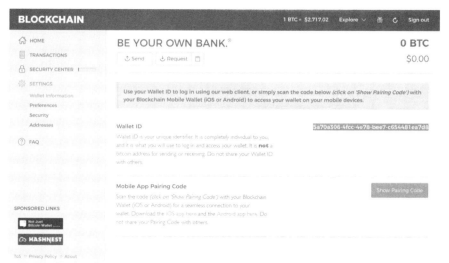

The next time you log in, you'll see two forms to fill in. Wallet ID and Password.

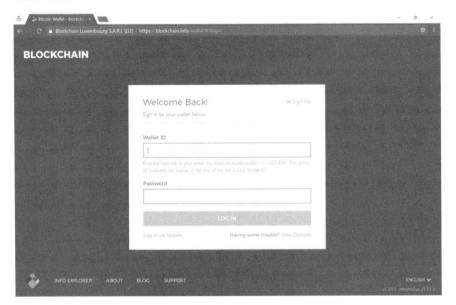

Now, once you're logged in, go to "Settings" and click on "Preferences" this time. Be sure to check your email and verify that. And then, if you wish, enable two-factor authentication using your mobile number. Meaning, before you log in, you must verify a code sent to your phone. (Not foolproof, but better than not doing it.)

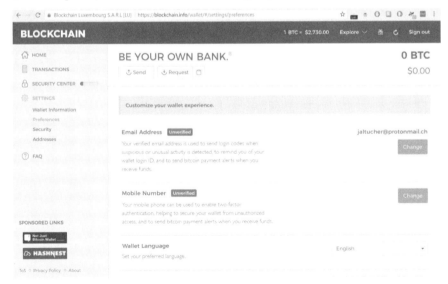

Once you're done there, click "**Security**." Check out the "**Wallet Recovery Phrase**." This phrase is a set of **12 randomly chosen words**. You'll need to record these words in the exact order they are given.

If you happen to lose your password, you can use these words (in this order) to recover your funds. It's a great back-up plan. Use it. Click "Backup Phrase."

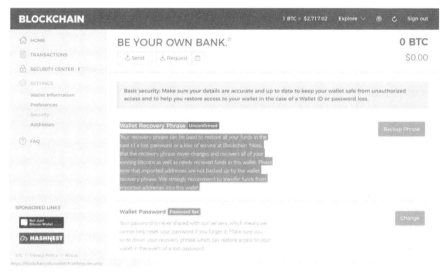

The words will show up four at a time. Write all of them down in a safe place. DO NOT store them on your computer.

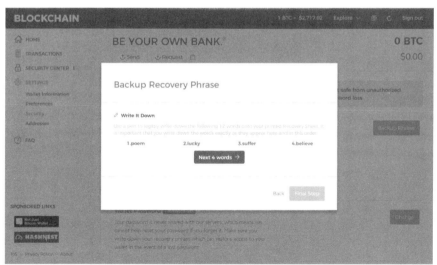

Once you've written them down in the correct order, you'll be asked to confirm you have the correct words in the correct order.

Finally, go to "Addresses" below "Security." You'll see the page below. Now click "Import Address."

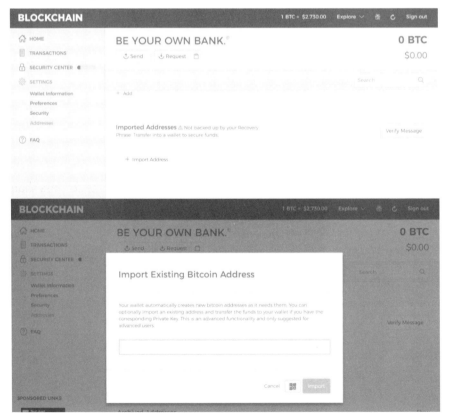

This is where you'll either type in your Private Key or scan your QR Code.

PARTIAL SPEND: IF YOU HAVE YOUR QR CODE

Use this function if you would like to keep some funds on the paper wallet.

1. Download Mycelium from the Android Play Store or through iTunes
2. Press the menu button and select "Cold Storage"
3. Scan in private key QR code or type it up, copy it and select "clipboard" to paste it
4. Select your destination address
5. Select the amount
6. Press the blue currency tag at the top to toggle currency
7. Send!

After spending, the private key in memory is destroyed so the paper private key remains secure.

[Even so, best practice is to be as paranoid as possible and immediately send the remaining balance to a paper wallet that was generated offline.]

COLD STORAGE DEVICES

There's also another less painful way to do all of this.

Simply get a cold storage device. You can get one online for less than $100 and they're specifically designed to be hack-proof.

The ones I recommend you check out are Trezor or a Ledger wallets. Unfortunately, they are currently limited to a few coins.

Both use state-of-the-art cryptographic technology to hold your private keys offline — even when the device is plugged into your computer.

Learn more about either on their websites:

Trezor: https://trezor.io/

Ledger: https://www.ledger.co/

(Ledger supports bitcoin, ethereum, ethereum classic, litecoin, dogecoin, zcash, dash and stratis)

CHAPTER 6:
THE NO. 1 CRYPTO TO BUY RIGHT NOW

The No. 1 crypto to buy, if I had to choose, is ethereum.

I'll tell you why I think it has such incredible potential. But please. Do your own due diligence.

As I'll explain in the next chapter, you shouldn't jump into any of these currencies without understanding what you're buying.

Cryptocurrencies have a purpose. Politically, they are built to help you gain independence of your life from institutional whim. You can cut out the middlemen. Someone in Brazil can pay someone in Switzerland without having to get permission from someone (or something) in New York City.

And furthermore, they're just the natural evolution of money. An evolution, as mentioned, theism to humanism to data-ism.

Bitcoin is the first sketch. We're going to find in the coming years that cryptocurrencies can do much more than just disrupt traditional banking — they have the potential to change the face of every industry on Earth. And I believe ethereum will lead the way.

ETHEREUM IS "BITCOIN 2.0"

Many ethereum fans call it "bitcoin 2.0."

Vitalik Buterin, the founder of ethereum, doesn't like it. He says it's like, "calling a smartphone a pocket calculator 2.0."

Henning Diedrich, author of *Ethereum*, says it's as wrong as calling "a calculator factor a calculator 2.0, because one can program something like bitcoin on top of ethereum."

I showed you some code earlier. I don't expect you to understand it. But this is what one of the most basic "contracts" on ethereum looks like. With this code, anyone can create a new cryptocurrency and set the initial supply in minutes.

```
contract MyToken {
        /* This creates an array with all balances */
        mapping (address => uint256) public balanceOf;

 /* Initializes contract with initial supply tokens to the creator of the
contract */
        function MyToken(
        uint256 initialSupply
        ) {
        balanceOf[msg.sender] = initialSupply; // Give the creator all
initial tokens
 }
        /* Send coins */
        function transfer(address _to, uint256 _value) {
        if (balanceOf[msg.sender] < _value) throw; // Check if the
sender has enough
        if (balanceOf[_to] + _value < balanceOf[_to]) throw; // Check
for overflows
        balanceOf[msg.sender] -= _value; // Subtract from the sender
        balanceOf[_to] += _value; // Add the same to the recipient
}
}
```

Once you deploy this contract and create your token, it's executed all over the world and made real on the blockchain. Everyone on the network must recognize it is real. And because nobody owns the network (in theory), there's no central command to destroy, block or censor your token from being created and used however you want.

So while bitcoin is focused on being a store of value and a currency, ethereum is focused on smart contracts and the construction of decentralized applications on the blockchain.

In **Chapter 3**, you might remember I said something about "contracts" without lawyers. The buzzword people use is "smart contracts," coined by programmer Nick Szabo (who might even be bitcoin's creator, Satoshi Nakamoto).

Here's the gist.

Law school 101 — Property and contract law are the fundamental building blocks of commercial society.

Smart contracts will allow us to enforce these aspects of society in a decentralized, "trustless" way. Our contracts become that fly in the amber I mentioned earlier.

Once set into the blockchain, they become immutable and unstoppable. Anything "signed" onto the blockchain becomes global and permanent. Moreover, data and programs are auditable by anyone.

This means…

A. It's impossible to renege on a "contract" or a decision once it's coded and set into motion on the blockchain.

B. Anyone can audit the blockchain and prove you did what you said you did.

Let's dig deeper into what a "smart contract" is to understand the implications.

SMART CONTRACTS

Nick Szabo, an interdisciplinary legal scholar, is the father of smart contracts. He wrote about them in the mid-'90s. Way before bitcoin. Way before ethereum.

I trust his definition of smart contracts:

"A smart contract is a set of promises, specified in digital form, including protocols within which the parties perform on these promises."

In an interview with Tim Ferriss, he says: "You can think of the primordial granddaddy of all smart contracts as the vending machine. So the vending machine in contract law terms, it verifies performance. You put in your quarter and it verifies you put in the quarter through its mechanical [slot]. I'm talking about the old-fashioned [ones]. It has logic in it that says OK, you put in a quarter, the soda costs a dime. So I'm going to give you a dime and a nickel back and the soda you selected."

The simplest form of a "smart contract" in cryptocurrency is a transaction on the bitcoin blockchain.

- James owes Jerry money in the form of bitcoin
- James uses bitcoin code to send a transaction
- Jerry receives bitcoin transaction code per agreement
- Code contract is fulfilled.

But smart contracts can go much further than that.

For example, with the help of these "smart contracts," according to Vitalik Buterin, "Ethereum can be used to codify, decentralize, secure and trade just about anything: voting, domain names, financial exchanges, crowdfunding, company governance, contracts and agreements of most kind, intellectual property, and even smart property thanks to hardware integration."

COLORED COINS

One potential use case is for ethereum to allow anyone to create their own "digital collectibles" for any purpose.

In his *Colored Coins* white paper, here's what Vitalik wrote:
The idea is to open up bitcoin as we know it now into two separate layers, being the underlying transactional network based on its cryp-

tographic technology and an overlay network of issuance of distinct instruments encapsulated in a design we call "colored coins."

If we can issue many distinct instruments within the bitcoin ecosystem, there are many potential use cases:

- A company might want to issue shares using colored coins, taking advantage of the bitcoin infrastructure to allow people to maintain ownership of shares and trade shares, and even allow voting and pay dividends over the bitcoin blockchain

- Smart property: suppose there is a car rental company. The company can release one colored coin to represent each car and then configure the car to turn on only if it receives a message signed with the private key that currently owns the colored coin. It can then release a smartphone app that anyone can use to broadcast a message signed with their private key and put up the colored coins on a trading platform. Anyone will be able to then purchase a colored coin, use the car for whatever period of time using the smartphone app as a "car key" and sell the coin again at their leisure

- A local community might wish to create a community currency using the bitcoin infrastructure to securely store funds

- A company may wish to create a corporate currency, such as Air Miles rewards points, or even plain coupons

- An issuer might wish to release a coin to represent deposits, allowing people to trade, for example, "Bitstamp-USD coins" or some gold storage company's "gold coins"

- Decentrally managing ownership of digital collectibles such as original artworks — just like art collectors buy and sell original copies of famous paintings for millions of dollars today, colored coins allow us to do the same with purely digital objects, such as songs, movies, e-books and software as well by storing the current ownership of the work as a colored coin on the blockchain.

THOUSANDS OF USE CASES

That said, there are thousands of potential use cases for ethereum.

Decentralized apps (dapps) could eat the world, run from the ethereum network. Think about Airbnb and Uber, which have already revolutionized their respective industries being run 100% P2P. Meaning, no middlemen to speak of.

Imagine, too, YouTube and Facebook becoming P2P, where the users get paid to show ads rather than a central commander sucking out all the value. (Digital plantations.)

Think:

Contracts… assets… shareholder agreements… prediction markets… voting systems… domain registries…

Peer-to-peer finance… derivatives… hedging… insurance…

Escrows… decentralized storefronts (censorship-resistant)… smart property… decentralized exchanges… savings accounts… wills… intellectual property…

ETHER TOKENS ARE THE FUEL FOR THE NETWORK

Without going too deep into the weeds, ethereum tokens are the "gas" fueling the ethereum network, an ecosystem of distributed applications.

It's a way to incentivize developers to build efficient, clean apps (wasteful code costs more ether) and that people are compensated for helping to run the network.

The more applications built on the ethereum network, the more valuable ethereum becomes.

It's the network effect on steroids.

And it just takes one killer dapp to make the ethereum network worth it. But I think there will be many.

CHAPTER 7:
THE #1 MISTAKE CRYPTOCURRENCY INVESTORS ARE MAKING

I'll keep this short, sweet and to the point.

My quick answer to which cryptocurrencies people should avoid is ALL of them.

Unless you're at least educated enough to know to look for those three things I spoke about in earlier chapters — and have them firmly implanted in your mind — you shouldn't invest a penny.

Remember, the (in theory) GOOD ones…

- Have a limited supply

- Fit with the cryptocurrency philosophy: secure (if James sends money to Joe, Joe gets it first and foremost), decentralized (no geographic borders), anonymous (nobody needs to know) and forgery-proof (no "duplicate money" is possible)

- Solve a problem that bitcoin doesn't already solve.

If they don't fit that criteria AT LEAST, run away.

HOW TO SPOT A SCAM

It's just a fact. In every boom market, there are always going to be scammers. It happened in the dot-com boom. Companies showing no profit went public — just to make the founders rich.

It happened in the housing boom, in which a lot of scammers got rich. And it's happening in the cryptocurrency boom.

At every turn, there's a new coin you can mine, a product to invest in, a crypto that promises incredible payouts. I promise you — they're mostly all scams. They are just land mines waiting for some fool to step on them.

The vast majority of coins you see on the market won't exist in five years. Most people can't see that. That's part of the reason why I've started writing about cryptocurrencies.

I'm tired of seeing good people getting scammed.

The thing is people hear about all of the great things cryptocurrencies can do and they get starry-eyed. They suspend their disbelief for the "hot new thing." They see a bitcoin millionaire teenager in the news and think it means they can become a millionaire in crypto, too.

Charlatans then rush in in droves. They tell people, "You've missed the boat on bitcoin but not on XXXCoin!" They give really complicated presentations that sound impressive but don't mean anything.

They use a lot of buzzwords like "decentralization" and "blockchain" and "trustless" without putting them in the proper context. They sound like geniuses to the laymen, but they're really stupid and very wrong. But many people just sit there and nod because they don't want to seem stupid themselves — and they want to believe what they are saying is true.

It's often said the difference between an entrepreneur and a scam artist is the former takes something simple and makes it very complex and the other takes something complex and makes it very simple.

The value can always be found in simplicity. Here's a general rule of thumb I like to stick to.

For what it's worth:

If it started with a massive premine (like, for example, DASH), I'd generally stay away.

If it's mined almost exclusively by a central authority (like, for example, STEEM), be wary.

If it doesn't solve any problems in the real world, it's not worth looking at.

If it claims to be able to solve MANY problems at once, it's probably hype.

And finally, if it doesn't have a strong community on social media or otherwise (Facebook, Twitter, Reddit, bitcointalk, Slack, Discord, etc.), then it's probably not going to go anywhere.

So I realize I didn't really give you a No. 1 crypto to avoid.

I didn't because giving you one currency just isn't a good enough answer. It's the wrong answer to the wrongheaded question.

The good answer is ALL OF THEM — until you're sure you know what you're looking at.

CHAPTER 8:
THE "VALUE-BASED" APPROACH TO *CRYPTO CORNER*

In the Crypto Corner, we're not going to focus so much on the cryptocurrencies themselves — but on the public plays.

That way, even if you have no intention of investing in the Wild West of crypto, you can still make incredible gains from crypto's rise.

That's right. You can invest in crypto from your regular old Fidelity account. And I'll give you a virtually foolproof way to invest in the crypto industry right here in this chapter.

First, though, let me give you the broad overview of how I view crypto investing. It's important you understand my perception if you plan to read any of my investment research.

VALUE-BASED INVESTING

I take a "value-based approach" to crypto.

You might ask: How do we estimate value in crypto? The same way any value investor would:

- Supply and demand, which are often determined by trustworthiness as well as usefulness. (e.g., you go into a McDonald's anywhere in the world and you trust that you will have the same experience. Plus, it solves a big problem — hunger). When supply and demand are temporarily misunderstood for identifiable, irrational reasons, this creates a trading opportunity

- Lots of reading, studying and talking to other trusted players in the space in order to make estimates on the above.

HOW TO BUILD A CRYPTO PORTFOLIO

We've gone through this a little bit in previous chapters but it's worth a quick refresher in this context.

A. To build a proper crypto portfolio, you must be able to determine which coins follow the pure cryptocurrency philosophy.

These legit coins belong in a diversified portfolio of cryptocurrencies. But it's VERY DIFFICULT to determine what's legit. *(See previous chapters for the more technical descriptions of these portfolio-worthy coins.)*

B. TRADES: Because of the great volatility as the world tries to determine intrinsic value for this brand new asset class, we can take advantage when volatility creates a big gap between current price and our estimation of value for each legit currency in the portfolio.

Why does volatility create opportunity? Because it's rare that intrinsic value changes very quickly from day to day.

Example: We know everything there is to know about McDonald's, and thousands of analysts research the company.

The intrinsic value of McDonald's will almost certainly never go down 20% in a day. But if the stock went down 20% in a day (example: A 9/11 event occurs, causing a mass-fear sell-off across all stocks), then McDonald's becomes a value buy because the volatility exceeded the normal change in value.

Volatility is a mainstay of the cryptocurrency world. And it presents plenty of opportunities for skilled traders to make money.

But in the *Crypto Corner*, I want us to focus on the basics — to go for the gains that are much more guaranteed over time.

THE NEW GOLD RUSH

In the Gold Rush, the pick and shovel companies thrived. Some people got rich on gold. And some didn't. And some found fool's gold.

But blue jeans thrived.

The same thing will happen here.

Chip companies, financial companies, retail companies, security companies and companies in every industry will have winners and losers in the crypto space.

The winners will go up many thousands of percent, regardless of what happens in the economy. In fact, a recession might even be good for these companies as people get nervous about their currency. It's no coincidence that the origin of cryptocurrencies occurred exactly at the moment that faith in the U.S. dollar was tested as a result of the financial crisis of 2008–09.

But what if this is all theory and cryptocurrencies take decades to get accepted by the masses?

No problem. Many of the companies that are "picks and shovels" in the cryptocurrency industry are, in fact, "picks and shovels"; i.e., they have many, many uses and are already successful companies.

I'll start with one example in this chapter.

Nvidia. (NASDAQ: NVDA)

Nvidia is known for making high-performance chips for computers specializing in games. Games require high-speed graphics and the chips to handle that.

Earlier I mentioned that in a cryptocurrency transaction, there are computers that specialize in validating transactions.

Some companies have thousands and thousands of computers set aside JUST to validate transactions.

Why? Because in bitcoin and another popular currency that I think is legitimate, ethereum, computers that validate transactions get rewarded in very controlled ways by making more coins for their efforts. These are called "miners" (the Gold Rush analogy again).

Miners benefit when their chips are fast. NVDA makes the chips that are most popular with miners right now.

So regardless of the economy, NVDA will sell more chips each year than the year before as the rise of cryptocurrencies continues on pace. Revenue growth is up 50% year over year and earnings growth is up 143% year over year. Good things are happening with this company regardless.

MY THREE-STEP SCRIPT FOR INVESTING IN THE CRYPTO BOOM

Did you know that **every single boom** throughout history has followed a three-step script?

The stock market boom in the roaring '20s…

The tech boom in the 1990s…

The housing boom in the 2000s…

And now the booming cryptocurrency market is following this exact same road map.

You see, every boom follows a sequence of three stages…

First, only early enthusiasts are courageous enough to invest in the new trend.

That's Stage 1.

Then, institutional investors (the so-called "smart money") jump in.

That's Stage 2.

Finally, the public joins the party, triggering a massive explosion in price.

That's Stage 3.

If you know how to use this road map, you could make an absolute fortune.

And to help you understand how this 1-2-3 sequence works…

Let me show you what happened during the 1990s boom in tech stocks.

In the mid-1990s, most people didn't even know what the internet was.

In 1994, NBC's morning show *Today* had a segment in which one of the anchors asked, "What is the internet anyway?"

While most people were dismissing the technology as a fad...

Early adopters were heavily investing in it.

That was Stage 1 of the boom!

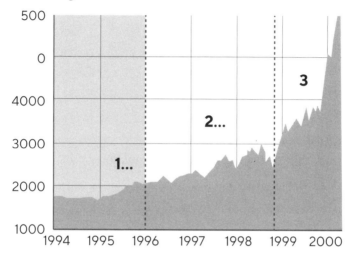

Only when Netscape went public in late 1995 did people outside Silicon Valley start taking the internet seriously.

That's when institutional investors started joining the party... with pension funds and venture capitalists making a fortune when companies like Yahoo and Amazon went public.

The additional flow of money from the "smart money" helped pushed tech stocks even higher.

That was Stage 2 of the boom.

But the public was still not participating.

In June 1998, for example, mainstream economist Paul Krugman predicted the internet's impact on the economy would be no greater than that of the fax machine.

It wasn't until 1999 that the masses finally started to invest heavily in tech stocks...

With more people jumping into the market...

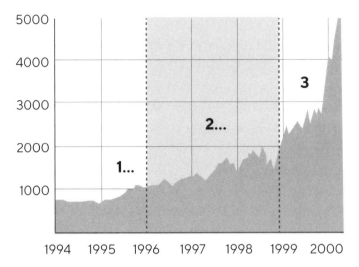

Tech stocks jumped even higher...

Attracting more and more people wanting to get a piece of the action.

And that was the third and most explosive stage of the boom...

With the Nasdaq soaring more than 85% in 1999 alone.

The 1-2-3 Script During the Tech Boom

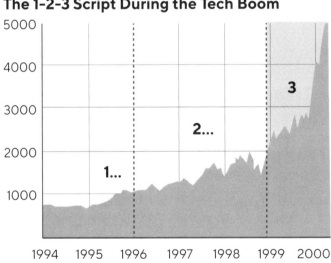

The so-called roaring '20s followed this same road map...

First, only early enthusiasts invested in the new technologies of the time, such as radio, the car and easy access to electric power.

Then in 1924, institutional investors jumped in…

Finally, in the late 1920s, the news started reporting stories of overnight fortunes.

And regular folks started to wonder: Why not me?

They started borrowing money just to buy stocks. The result?

Stocks went straight up. In 1928 alone, the stock market doubled.

The 1-2-3 Script During the Roaring '20s

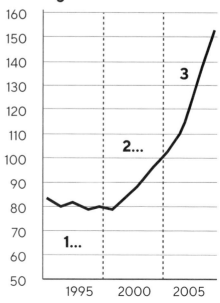

And it's not just stocks. The U.S. housing boom also followed this script…

Take a look…

The biggest jump in housing prices happened from 2003–06…

When we entered Stage 3 of the boom… and flipping houses became a national obsession:

And it's not just in the U.S.

Something similar happened during the historic boom in Japanese stocks…

The 1-2-3 Script During the Housing Boom

With the masses pushing stocks straight up during Stage 3 in the 1980s.

This script is so reliable that it goes back centuries...

Just look what happened with shares of the South Sea Co. in 1720.

And with the boom in tulip bulbs in Holland during the early 1600s.

Isn't that incredible?

No matter what asset class...

No matter the geographic location...

And no matter what year the boom happened...

Every single boom throughout history has followed the same script.

It works 100% of the time.

And in each one of those booms, people who knew how to use this script walked away with a fortune.

Those who didn't lost all their money.

I'm telling you all this because this script is playing out again RIGHT NOW in the booming cryptocurrency market!

So where are we now in this digital currency boom?

Let me you walk you through the three stages using bitcoin as an example...

The 1-2-3 Script During the Japanese Boom

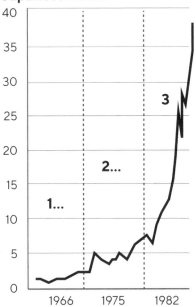

The 1-2-3 Script in the South Sea Company

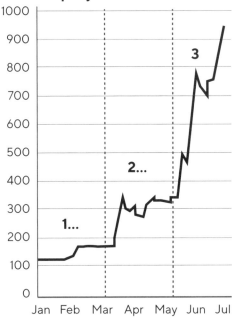

The 1-2-3 Script in the Tulip Boom

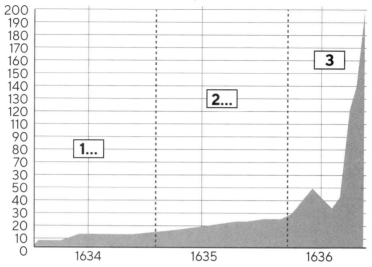

When bitcoin "went public" in 2010, very few people understood the opportunity.

Much like the internet in 1994, most people dismissed it as a useless technology.

Only early enthusiasts invested in bitcoin…

That was Stage 1 of the boom.

We've moved into Stage 2 around 2014…

When institutional investors, aka "the smart money," started investing in bitcoin.

And what started in 2014 has only intensified in 2017.

You see, the "smart money" is not just looking at bitcoin anymore.

With hundreds of cryptocurrencies exploding 3,475%, 21,611% and even 81,465%…

They're now investing in these smaller, lesser-known digital currencies.

Forbes even published the following headline recently…

"Crypto Boom: 15 New Hedge Funds Want in on 84,000% Returns"

And went on to report:

"Given how many new crypto-millionaires have been minted… old hands in finance who want in on this new world of value are launching funds."

Aside from these 15 new hedge funds…

There are 70 more in the pipeline!

Once all these 70 funds get set up, billions of new capital will flow into these cryptocurrencies…

Helping push them even higher.

And get this…

Fidelity, which has $6.2 trillion in assets under management, has just partnered with Coinbase, the most popular cryptocurrency exchange.

Imagine what will happen if some of those trillions start moving into cryptos!

Remember, this is all part of Stage 2 of my three-step script.

And to prove my point, here's an inside scoop…

Andreessen Horowitz and Sequoia Capital are two of the most highly respected venture capital firms in Silicon Valley.

That's because they tend to see major technology trends before anyone else.

They've made billions by investing very early in social media companies like Facebook, LinkedIn and Twitter.

Simply put, when these guys invest in something new, you should pay close attention.

Well, right now, they're secretly investing in a cryptocurrency fund called MetaStable.

How do I know that?

Because I'm good friends with one of the founders of the fund.

You see, in the last 30 years, I've built connections that go from the head of Google X (Google's experimental laboratory)…

to Peter Thiel, founder of PayPal and early investor in Facebook …

to billionaire Mark Cuban, owner of the Dallas Mavericks and *Shark Tank* TV show star.

Because of my connections, I can see behind the scenes that the "smart money" is now getting heavily involved in cryptocurrencies.

Mark Cuban is planning to get involved…

Google is investing in it… and so is billionaire Richard Branson.

Look, I recently had lunch with several hedge fund managers and other "Wall-Streeters" in New York…

And they wanted to give me $50 million to start a new crypto hedge fund. I declined their offer. Why? Because I'd have to give up doing the things I love, such as writing my blogs, this book, my newsletter *The Altucher Report*… and my podcast.

Those are the things I love to do. And no amount of money in the world can make me give it all up.

But I'm telling you this story simply to prove to you that the "smart money" want to get involved in cryptos… because they know this is a once-in-a-generation opportunity.

BUT WHILE THE "SMART MONEY" IS GOING ALL IN… EVERYDAY FOLKS ARE TOTALLY IN THE DARK

Despite the massive investments from "the smart money"…

Despite all the newly minted millionaires…

And despite this exploding market…

Most people don't even know what a cryptocurrency is.

To this date, fewer than one in 10,000 people have invested in bitcoin.

Just ask your friends, spouse and neighbors what they think of ethereum, litecoin and monero.

I bet they'll have no clue what you're talking about.

That's because the masses are NOT participating in this boom.

Not yet!

Professor Panos Mourdoukoutas, chair of the department of economics at Long Island University in New York, agrees with me.

He says we're still missing "a broad participation beyond the 'pioneers' and the 'early adopters.'"

And that's the key to my three-step script.

Remember, the biggest gains in any bull market throughout history only happen when the public joins the trend.

It's the masses that will push cryptocurrencies to the moon.

That means these digital currencies still have a lot of upside potential. With cryptocurrencies minting new millionaires seemingly every day… This epic boom is starting to grab some headlines.

Take a look…

The Guardian writes, "The booming market in… cryptocurrencies… could now be on the cusp of mainstream financial credibility."

And billionaire investor Michael Novogratz: "There's so much human capital and real money being poured into the space and we're at the takeoff point."

CNBC trader Brian Kelly: "Cryptocurrencies are following the same exponential growth trajectory as the internet. "It's a **once-in-a-generation investment opportunity.**"

And Henry Blodget, founder of Business Insider, says: "There is **infinite upside.**"

With cryptocurrencies gaining publicity…

The masses will NOT remain on the sidelines for much longer.

That's why it's important you get started as soon as possible.

And there's a single event that could catapult cryptos into the third and most explosive phase of the boom.

Simply put, this event will trigger a buying frenzy…

And help mint a new round of crypto millionaires.

You see, big tech companies like Microsoft and Overstock are already accepting bitcoin as a form of payment.

But what would happen if the world's largest online retailer started doing the same?

We're about to find out…

Because with the popularity of bitcoin exploding…

With people like Bill Gates saying cryptocurrencies are "the future of money"…

And with big economies like Japan's legalizing bitcoin as a form of payment…

Amazon WILL accept bitcoins as a form of payment.

And they could make an announcement anytime.

EBay, Amazon's biggest competitor, has already expressed interest in accepting bitcoin payment.

And according to Overstock CEO Patrick Byrne, Amazon will soon have no choice but to start accepting bitcoins. He said:

"They have to follow suit… I'll be stunned if they don't because they can't just cede that part of the market to us, if we're the only main, large retail site taking bitcoin."

Look, Amazon Web Services has already been working with Digital Currency Group, one of the biggest investors in the cryptocurrency technology.

And Amazon executive Scott Mullins has confirmed it…

Amazon is "working with financial institutions and [crypto experts] to spur innovation and facilitate frictionless experimentation."

Once they make this announcement, the impact on cryptocurrencies will be huge.

We'll see a buying frenzy like never before. It'll be like a Black Friday crowd at Best Buy.

Only those who get in early will get a good deal. Most people will be left out. That's why I urge you to get in right now. Get ahead of the massive buying frenzy that will push cryptocurrencies straight up.

Like I showed you today, every boom follows this three-step script. First, only early adopters bought bitcoin. Then, the smart money started joining the party. And now we're about to enter the third and most explosive stage of the boom in cryptocurrencies.

That's why I wrote this book. To help you get started before it's too late.

BONUS CHAPTER: HOW TO INVEST IN BITCOIN FROM YOUR RETIREMENT ACCOUNT

There are two ways you can invest in bitcoin from your retirement account. One is so absurd I have to mention it in this chapter. The other is worth checking out.

Typically, IRA custodians accept only mainstream assets. These include stocks, bonds, mutual funds, CDs, etc.

A bitcoin IRA isn't linked to any systemic risk that affects ALL other mainstream IRA investments. If it all falls down, it's best to have your risk spread into "off Wall (Street)" investments.

Your best option for including bitcoin into your retirement fund is a self-directed IRA. When you do this, you can buy and hold bitcoins or buy shares of bitcoin-dedicated funds. (I prefer the former over the latter.)

If you want to allocate some of your retirement funds through a self-directed IRA, you have two options:

1. For the DIYers who are masochists at heart, you can set up an LLC for IRS compliance.

This involves setting up an LLC for your bitcoins, wading through all of the rules and red tape, selling your bitcoin, contributing the money to the IRA and then buying it in the name of the LLC with its own assets.

This is a laughably insane way to go about investing in bitcoin and I don't suggest it. After all, this is precisely the kind of thing bitcoin was created to make obsolete.

2. Try out Bitcoin IRA.

BitcoinIRA helps people roll over their retirement funds to bitcoin and secure their coins in cold storage, facilitated by BitGo (they provide secure wallet services).

If you're interested in rolling over some of your retirement funds into bitcoin, it's worth the commission. Otherwise, you'll be wading through a swamp of compliance issues and absurd hoops.

And we'll all laugh at you.

Check it out here at **www.bitcoinIRA.com**

NOTES:

NOTES:

NOTES: